BEING CUBAN!

Grandma's

"dicharachos"

By Pilar Pelayo Paz

DEDICATION

I dedicate this book to my MOM Miriam and sister Rosemary, my Aunt Selma, my maternal grandmother Abuela Nana, my paternal grandmother Abuela Julia, Chicha Oliver, and the illustrious Guillermo Alvarez Guedes for cradling and comforting us in our exile with his unparalleled humor, and to all my fellow Cuban immigrants that came to the U.S. at a young age. We were fortunate to live and grow up with our grandparents and elders who taught us these "dicharachos" that are now in danger of being lost and forgotten. It is my intention to keep them alive and pass them on. ENJOY!!!

TABLE OF CONTENTS

Chapter 1

Why this book now

So why this book now? Because we're losing it! If you're like me, you either came to the U.S. at a very early age, or were born here relatively soon after your parents arrived. This wave of immigration of ours was both delighted to be here and become "Americanized", as well as deeply nostalgic with a great sense of loss. One of the most common things to say, which became a joke over time, was that whatever "it" was, was better in Cuba.

Our grandparents' generation had the toughest time adjusting, never really integrating, much less learning to speak English. Our parents, on the other hand, were more invested in their new lives in the U.S. They managed to learn English, as best they could, wanting to progress right away, and make the most out of life here for themselves and their children.

It was a magical time! We, as kids, also had to learn a new language AND QUICK! Lest be subjected to ridicule. Thankfully, we did! So much so that we spoke only English at home after a while. We soon figured out it was a great way to say anything in front of some of the adults and they wouldn't understand a word. It did become common that those of us who hadn't gotten a good grasp of Spanish, having left Cuba too young, were losing the language to some extent. That not being the better part of wisdom, led to the "no English in the house" rule. It was the best thing for us, really, since we did salvage our

Spanish, especially these following words and expressions of the ages that we grew up with and hardly ever hear much anymore, let alone use ourselves. My mom is almost forgetting herself! I called around some friends and older relatives to help me approximate the spelling as much as possible. But lo and behold, no one had heard most of this stuff in so long, let alone written or read it, that no one was really sure.

Please forgive any discrepancies you may find.

Some translations are accurate, some are approximations, and some are just literal translations, because I couldn't find a way to interpret those at all. Every time I thought I was finished, I thought of something else! There may be a bunch more I remember after all this. I hope not. I hope I have most in here. All in all, this is a pretty good list. Enjoy it! Share it!

Chapter 2

Grandma's "Words"

A

Abollado - dented; dent; misshapen

Acoquinado - sheepish; chagrined; forlorn

Aguacero - heavy rain shower

Aguafiesta - killjoy

Ajetreo - rushing; too busy

Alarde / Alardoso - bluff; show off; brag

Alboroto / Alborotado - commotion; excitement; rambunctious

Alcaueta - matchmaker; meddler

Alebrestado – riled up; rambunctious

Amaguyado – lumpy; dented; beat up

Andancio – Malaise; cold or flu

Apolizmado – Bruised; beat up; dented

Apurruñado – squeezed too tightly in a hug

Arretranco – Big piece of junk

Asomate – look out the door or window

Aspaviento – huff and puff

Atarugado – Overstuffed; choking; gagging

Atascado - stuck

Atestado – thrown together and stuffed

Atollado / Atolladera - stuffed tightly; too much

Atolondrado - bewildered; confused

Atosigado - Overwhelmed; cornered; gasping

Aura tiñosa - vulture; someone always negative

B

Babero - bib

Batea - laundry sink with washboard

Bemba - lips; mouth

Biruta - piece of debris; undefined lump

Blumer - women's and girl's underwear

Boberia - nonsense

Bobo - dumb; silly

Bochinche - gossiping

Bocon - big mouth

Bombo - bland; lukewarm

Brete / Bretero - brawl; altercation; instigator

Boronilla - crumbs

Burundanga - miscellanaous stuffing

C

Cacharro - junky car or container

Cachicambiado - mangled; dented

Cachumbambe - seesaw

Cagalera - diarrhea

Cagalitroso - decrepit

Cantaleta - nagging; whining

Carriola - skate board with wheels and handle

Ceboruco - lumpy; crude object; dumbass

Chambelona - lollipop

Chancleta - flipflop; sandal

Chapapote - tar

Chinatas - marbles

Chiquero - pig stye; wet dirty floor

Chiringa - small kite

Chisme - gossip

Chismosa - gossip-y

Chivaton - snitch

Chorro - stream of water or fluid

Chucho - electrical outlet; light switch

Chusma - lowlife; low class; vulgar in speech

Cojonudo - has balls

Colorete - blush; rouge

Comebola - *polite version of 'comemierda'*

Comecatibia - *idiot*

Comemierda - *super idiot; jackass; asshole*

Contrapunteo - *constant bickering*

Cucaracha - *holes in a bad haircut*

Cucurucho - *pointy hat; cone-like object*

Culero - *diaper*

Culicagao - *a kid; too young to be acting older*

Cuquear - *tease; coax*

D

Desaforada - unbridled frenzy

Descojonado - tired; exhausted; fucked up

Desconflautado - falling apart; misshapen

Desgañitandose - screaming wildly

Desguazado - pulled or torn apart

Desguavinado - exhausted; beat

Desmoñingado - twisted apart; disheveled

Despelusado - ruffled; messy hair; bad haircut

Despetroncado - stampeding; tripping over feet

Despilfarrado - shredded apart; torn; gnarled

Despojo - spiritual cleansing

Destutanado - exhausted

Desvencijado - rumpled; falling apart; caving in

E

Embarcado - stood up; left behind; in the lurch

Embarrado - dirty; smeared with dirt

Embarre - a dirty mess; a big mix up

Empedernido - exagerated in some way

Empercudido - filthy dirty; grimy

Emperifollado - excessive jewelry and adornment

Encartonado - stiff; pasty dry skin

Encascarillada - powdery face

Encasquetado - crammed down; stuffed in

Encojido - shrunken; shriveled

Engurruñado - crumpled; wrinkled

Enjillado - sunken in; gangly

Entizado - wrapped heavily and haphazardly

Escabullirse - sneak out

Escaparate - armoire; cabinet

Escatimando - shortchanging; cutting corners

Escusao - outhouse pit

Esmirriado - wimpy; saggy

Estenuado - exhausted

F

Fañoso – nasaly; stuffy nose sounding

Farolero – rambunctious; solicitous

Ferretreque – "party"; carousing

Fina – well mannered; proper etiquette

Fletera - slut

Fondillo – butt

G

Galleta / Galletazo - slap

Gangarrías - excessive, gawdy jewelry

Garnaton - hard slap

Gaseñiga - type of loaf cake with raisins

Gofío - ground toasted wheat

Grajo - underarm odor; "b.o."

Greñas - droopy, scanty, messy hair

Grillo malojero - twirp

Guagua - bus

Guajiro - country bumpkin; "shy"

Guanajo - "turkey"; fool

Guaricandilla - slutty girl; chusma; rifraff

Guasabeo - syrupy flirtation; mutual tease

Guataca - ear; brown nose

Guayabera - classic Cuban man's shirt

H

Huesito de la alegría - tail bone

Huevon - lazy; slacker; dim wit

I

(none...?)

J

Jabao - mulatto with light colored hair

Jamonero - fresh guy always feeling up women

Jediondo - dirty; disgusting

Jelengue - game; mess; nonsense; fooling around

Jeringar - to annoy

Jeringonza - speaking gibberish

Jicotea - turtle

Jigote - thick blob

Jimaguas - twins

Jiña - resentment, or "bullshit"

Jiribilla – restlessness; fidgety

Jodedor – prankster; playboy

Jodedera – fooling around; nuisance

Jorobeteado – bad posture; twisted; mangled

Julepe – hustle and bustle

K

(none...?)

L

Ladilla - annoying

Lio - problem; mess; altercation

M

Machucado - dealt with; more or less

Majadero - cranky

Majomía - nagging obsessive-compulsively

Mamarracho - sloppily or gawdily dressed

Mameyazo - bump to the head

Manganzon - slacker, spoiled mama's boy

Maraña - trick or underhanded business

Maroma - playful; silly physical antics

Marindango - disliked "boyfriend"

Marrullero - "alley" cat

Mataperreando - running around on the streets

Matraquilla - repetitive nagging

Mejunge - undefinable mix of ingredients

Melindroso - finicky; diminutive

Mentecato - fool; poor decision maker; idiot

Mequetrefe - imbecil; ordinary substandard guy

Metiche - meddler

Mirringoso - scanty; miserly amount

Moneria - something cute; goofy

Monisima - adorable

Mueca - making a "face"

Murumaca - similar to 'maroma'

Murruñoso - mangy, dreary; disheveled; drippy

N

Niño bitongo - mama's boy

Ñ

Ñame - (root vegetable); dumb

Ñandu - derrogatory for a simpleton

Ñangueteada - physically impaired; crippled

Ñañara - undefined skin wound

Ñoño / Ñoña - pouty; whinny; needing TLC

O

Ojeroso – bags under the eyes

P

Palangana – water basin; pan

Palo – stiff drink; shot of alcohol; stick

Pan con timba – simple sandwich

Papalote – kite

Parapete – screen; object dividing space

Parejera – cute and frivolous in attire

Patatus - sudden collapse; heart attack

Patitieso - stiff; cold and stale

Patizambo - bow-legged

Pejiguera - always the same annoying nagging

Pelagato - poor; no money or property

Pendejo - coward

Perilla - button; small protrusion

Pezcozon - hard pinch on the neck and ear

Pinpanpun - folding portable bed or cot

Piñazo - punch in the face

Pisicorre - "pisa y corre" = station wagon

Pitifeo - ugly; diminutive and homely

Potaje – thick, chunky soup

Presumida – always made-up and dressed-up

Pujo – trying to be funny; bad joke

Piruli – pointy cone -shaped lollipop

Q

Quisquilloso - finicky; fastidious

R

Rabadilla - lower back

Raquítico - too small; underdeveloped

Rebijía - too young and undergrown

Recoveco - winding; meandering narrow path

Refunfuñando - muttering; mumbling grumpily

Regodeo - taking too long; procrastinating

Reguilete - hand-size paper windmill

Relambia – conceited and precocious

Rellollo - fat

Resabioso – ornery; grumpy

Retozando – playing rambunctiously

Retuzando – short-changing; stingy rationing

Rollizo - fat

Ronco – hoarse

Roña – resentment; ire; fury

S

Sabichoso - smart alleck

Safia - malicious and ensnaring

Salla - skirt

Salluela - underskirt

Sanguijuela - obnoxious little sucker

Sato - mutt; flirt

Sicatera - cheap; stingy

Sicote - foot odor

Sigilio - nagging conundrum

Siju platanero - little and quirky

Sobaco - armpit

Solar - ghetto housing

Sombrilla - umbrella; parasol

Sonsacando - luring; coaxing

Sube y Baja - café con leche; latte

Surcir - mend a hole by sewing

T

Taburete- stool

Tambaleandose - stumbling

Tambucho - container

Tareco - piece of junk

Tarugo - plug; short squatty object

Tayuyo - wearing ill-fitting clothes; tamal without meat

Tete - pacifier

Tembleque - shaking; tremors

Tibor - chamber pot

Timbiriche - crappy food stand

Tisico - emaciated; scrawny

Titere - clownish; tacky dresser

Toqueteo - fondling & groping

Tolete - dumb; a stick

Tolondron - sloppy lump

Tortica de moron - macaroon-like dry cookie

Traqueteado - beat up; damaged

Traquimaña - shady deal; cheating

Trocado - confused

Tuburio - bad neighborhood

Tumbadero - delapidated housing

Turulata - senile; feeble minded

U

Ule - plastic sheet or tarp

V

Vago - lazy

Veintiunico - the only one

Velocipido - tricycle

Verija - crotch

W

(none...?)

X

(none...?)

Y

Yaya / Yayai - "boo boo"; scrape; wound

Z

Zangano - lazy; slacker; mama's boy

Zangaleton - derivative of "zangano"

Zangandongo - also derivative of zangano

Zarro - crust; dirty residue; "schmootz"

Zoquete - stupidly stubborn; beligerant

Chapter 3

Grandma's " dicharachos"

(descriptive)

A la buena de Dios - slow in coming along; slow paced

A la cañona - coherce by force

A la hora de los mameyes - at the end of the day

A las mil y quinientas - very late

A lo loco - wrecklessly

A millon - full speed ahead

A ojo de buen Cubero - eye balling it more or less

A santo de que? - why on earth...?

A todo lo que da - full speed; all the way

A todo meter - same as above; full speed ahead

A troche y moche - done sloppily and excessively

A tutiplen - all over the place; left and right

Al hilo - on the straight and narrow

Al retortero - dragging something around always

Alabado sea Dios! - Oh my God!

Alla tu! - at your own risk

Alla va eso! - there goes nothing!

Alto como una vara de tumbar cocos - very tall

Arroz con mango - a mess

Así cualquiera - having it easy; advantage

Blanco en canas - grey haired

Brilla por su ausencia - nowhere to be seen

Calvo como una bola de billar - totally bald

Candil de la calle, oscuridad de la casa - nice to strangers, jerk at home

Cara de "yo no fui" - "wasn't me" face

Como cosa tuya - as if coming from YOU

Como el que no quiere la cosa - in a sneaky way

Como Pedro por su casa - making one self at home; walking in unannounced

Como quiera - sloppily; carelessly

Como rinde! - relentlessly overly active

Como seis en un zapato - uncomfortable; not feeling well

Como un matrimonio mal llevado - heavy; cumbersome

Como una suela de zapato - hard as shoe leather

Como una ternera en feria - wearing too much jewelry

Con disimulo - tactfully; slyly

Con el moco caído - down in the dumps

Con el cuento y la jarana - between one thing and another

Con la lengua afuera - panting; out of breath

Dar el visto bueno - give a blessing; approval

De buenas a primeras - all of a sudden

De eso nada monada - no way!

Del año de Ñañasere - ancient

De Pascua a San Juan - once in a blue moon

De película - like a movie; exaggerated

Diera lo que no tengo… - I'd give anything…

Dolor del guajiro /guaguero - brain freeze

Donde el diablo dio las tres voces - far;
bumfuck Egypt

Donde se hace la cruz? - "well, well, well..."

Dos pies izquierdos - two left feet; can't dance

El diablo y la capa - the whole kit and kaboodle

El mismo que viste y calza - one and the same

En clenque - old and weak

En el dime que te dire - arguing back and forth

En el pico de la piragua - up high; at some
altitude

En la lucha - frenzy of making a living

En la luna de Valencia - *absentminded; daydreaming*

En un abrir y cerrar de ojos - *in the blink of an eye*

En un 2 por 3 - *swiftly and quickly*

Envuelto en llamas - *in big trouble*

Encuero en pelota - *totally naked*

Entre la espada y la pared - *between a rock and a hard place*

Entre pitos y flautas - *rigamarole*

Es candela - *mischievous; clever; rambunctious*

Es el colmo - *the last straw; over the top*

Es la pata del diablo - *same as 'es candela'*

Es un monstruo - very talented or good looking

Ese enfermo esta grave - something broken

Eso no se da todos los dias - rare; unique

Frio como la pata de un muerto - cold & stiff

Gatica Maria Ramos tira la piedra y esconde la mano - sneaky; underhanded; pretending to be innocent

Habian tres gatos - very few people; almost empty

Hasta la coronilla - having "had it up to here"!

Hasta que el manco eche dedos - keep going on and on

La estampa de la eregia - looking gaunt and emaciated

Le vino como anillo al dedo - perfect fit; exactly what was needed

Le vino de perilla - same as above; convenient

Lo nunca visto - unbelievable; shocking

Lo que ve la suegra - marginally clean

Loco de remate - completely crazy

Mal de Sambito - quirky twitch

Mas o menos - more or less

Mas viejo que andar a pie - older than dirt

Mas viejo que Matusalen - same as above

Menos mal - thank goodness

Mira a ver! - look out; be careful

Mismo perro diferente collar - same dog, different collar

Mosquita muerta - sweet and innocent façade

Muerto de hambre - poor; having nothing

Muerto en vida - looking gaunt; on the verge of death

Muy conocido en su casa - a nobody

Naricita huele peo - small, upturned nose

Negro como un toti - blacker than black

No doy mas - done; exhausted

No hay moros en la costa - the coast is clear

No puede ni con su alma - weak and frail

No tiene ni donde amarrar la chiva - doesn't have a pot to piss in or a window to throw it out of

No tiene ni donde caerse muerto - same as above

No vale ni la cagada de un borracho - worthless

Ojos de ternero degollado - droopy, wistful eyes

Oscuro como la boca de un lobo - dark as night

Oscuro y huele a queso - same as above

Oyo campanas y no sabe donde - can't get the story straight and starts a rumor

Pagar el pato - to take the blame

Pelado a la malanguita - boy buzz cut

Pelado a moñito - very short haircut

Pelado a mordidas - bad haircut

Pelado con vidrio - same as above

Peo mal tirado - small person; twirp

Perdona el poco caso - being ignored

Pidiendo el agua por señas - destitute

Que bien se ve... - sarcastically implying the obvious

Que mojon! - a drag; extremely annoying

Que se va a hacer...? - oh well...; what are you gonna do...?

Que te parece...? - how do you like that?

Que va! - no way!

Rojo como un tomate - red cheeked; blushing

Se cayo de la cama - woke up unusually early

Se las trae - someone to be reckoned with

Se le pegaron las sabanas - overslept

Se levanto con el moño virado - woke up cranky; in a bad mood

Se levanto con el pie izquierdo - got off on the wrong foot; day is going badly

Se me quedo en una muela - very small portion of food

Se puso las botas - "scored"

Se salvo - got lucky

Sigue durmiendo de ese lado - keep thinking
that way

Sin ir mas lejos... - quick pertinent anecdote

Sin plumas y cacareando - left with nothing

Sin ton ni son - without heads or tails

Tal para cual - two peas in a pod

Tamal mal envuelto - dressed in ill-fitting
clothes

Tapon de bañadera - short and squatty person

Te la comiste - you did a great job

Tiene la boca cuadrada - gets left out

Un pollo de cada gallo - each kid from a different father

Un gustazo un trancazo - self inflicted wound

Va que te tumbos - clonky, heavy shoes

Viejo cañengo - decrepit old man

Ya tu sabes! - you know what's coming...

Yegua desenfrenada - frantic woman

(action...)

A _(verb, i.e. comer,...)_ se ha dicho! - to embark upon an activity full force.

Acabo como la fiesta del guatao - ended in a brawl or fight

Bateo de home run - ate all the food on plate

Buscale la foto de la abuela - looking for the family traits

Buscando por donde le entra el agua al coco - scrutinizing something carefully

Buscandole las tres patas al gato - looking for trouble

Cogiendo mango bajito - having it too easy

Dando lata – overstaying welcome; not knowing when to stop or leave

Dando palique – talking too much

Dando zanzara – running around

Dar la vuelta a la manzana – walk around the block

Dar una vuelta de carnera – cartwheel

Desvestir un santo para vestir otro – borrowing from Dick to pay Harry

Esta acabando – doing well; learning fast; wreaking havoc

Estan en el quita y pon – going back and forth

Estiro la pata – died

Haciendose de la vista gorda – pretending not to see something

Haciendo de las suyas - up to his old tricks

Haciendo de tripas corazon - making the best of a situation

Hay hasta para hacer dulce - excessive amount available

Hay que tener gandinga - gotta have gall; temerity

Jugando de manos - rough housing

Lavate la papeleta - a whore's bath

Le puso la tapa al pomo - the last straw

Le salio el tiro por la culata - backfired

Le viene como anillo al dedo - perfect fit

Le viene de perilla - hits the spot

Lloviendo a cantaros - pouring rain

Mandalo a freir tuzas - send him to hell

Mandalo pal carajo - same as above

Matar dos pajaros de un tiro - kill two birds
with one stone

Me cago en la madre de los tomates - "I shit
on the mother of the tomatoes"; you figure it out...

Metele mano - take it; get into it; "hit" it

Meter la Habana en Guanabacoa - stuff 2 lbs
of bologne in a 1 lb bag

Meterse en camisa de 11 baras - asking for
trouble

Murio de algo malo - died of something "bad"

Murio de repente - died suddenly

No dijo ni pio - didn't say a word

No pinta nada ahi - has no business there

Partele el brazo - seal the deal

Pasando las de Cain - struggling

Pasando mas trabajo que un forro de catre - struggling; going through hell

Pensando en las musarañas - head up in the clouds; daydreaming

Prometiendo villas y castillas - writing checks you can't cash

Que se traen entre manos? - what are you up to?

Quedo en la ultima pagina - *eliminated*

Quererse tirar los peos mas altos que el culo - *wanting to live beyond their means*

Quien te manda? - *shouldn't have done that; told you so*

Quieren estar en misa y en procesion - *wanting to be in two places at once*

Revento como un siquitraqui - *exploded loudly*

Salio de fuego a entrar en incendio - *out of the fire into the frying pan*

Salio de Guatemala a Guatepeor - *from bad to worse*

Salpica para alla - *move over; get away*

Se alboroto gusanera - *got riled up*

Se callo redondo - fell or collapsed suddenly

Se formo un sal pa fuera - skirmish; "everybody out!"

Se le fue la guagua - "missed the boat"

Se le fue por el camino viejo - went down the wrong pipe

Se lleno la boca - boasted; spoke too soon

Se salvo de un tilin - saved by the bell

Te peinas o te haces papelillos - make up your mind

Tirando la casa por la ventana - sparing no expense; going way over budget

Tocame Roque, no me toques Roque - can't decide; going back and forth

Venir a bailar a casa del trompo - wanting to reinvent the wheel

Chapter 4

Grandma's "wisdom"

A caballo regalado no se le miran colmillos - can't look a gift horse in the mouth

A mí que no me vengan con cuento - can't fool me

Al pan pan y al vino vino - call a spade a spade

Cada cual se la come a su manera - to each his own

Cada loco con su tema - same as above

Con estos bueyes hay que halar - this is what you have to work with

Cortando huevos se aprende a capar - practice makes perfect

Cuando el mal es de cagar no valen guayabas verdes - when it rains, it pours

Dando y dando - give and take; even Steven

Dios aprieta pero no ahoga - God gives you nothing you can't handle

Donde manda capitan no manda soldado - Too many chiefs, not enough Indians

El hambre aprieta - hunger compels or motivates

El muerto al hoyo y el vivo al pollo - the dead to the hole, the living to the bowl

El mundo es un pañuelo - it's a small world

El pescado muere por la boca - the fish dies through the mouth

El que da lo que tiene a pedir se queda - *if you give away what you have you end up having to borrow...*

El que le roba a un ladron tiene cien años de perdon - *who steals from a thief has 100 years pardon*

El que no oye consejo no llega a viejo - *a word to the wise...*

El que quiere comer pescado se tiene que mojar el culo - *if you want the fruit you have to climb the tree*

El que rie ultimo rie mejor - *see who gets the last laugh*

El que se acuesta con niños amanece cagao - *one who sleeps with kids wakes up full of shit*

El que se la fume pierde el vicio - *whoever smokes her will quit cold turkey*

En boca cerrada no entran moscas - *closed mouth gathers no moths*

Eramos pocos y pario la abuela - as if we didn't have enough

Escobita nueva barre bien - new broom gets all the dust... the new one is always better at first

Eso no se lo cree ni el medico chino - no one will believe that in a million years

Esta como Mamiola. si se la meten grita y si se la sacan llora - damned if you do, damned if you don't

Guerra avisada no mata soldados - forewarned is forearmed

Hay ayudas que merecen palos - better no help than bad help

La cabra tira al monte - the apple doesn't fall far from the tree

La ley del pobre, reventar antes que sobre - the poor finish everything on their plate

La luz de alante es la que alumbra - bird in hand is better than two in the bush

La necesidad hace parir mulatos - necessity is the mother of invention

Le ronca el mango /merequeten/moño - exclamation of extreme annoyance; unbelievable!

Llueve sobre lo mojado - beating a dead horse

Lo barato sale caro - there are no free lunches

Lo que no mata engorda - that which doesn't kill you makes you stronger

Los niños hablan cuando las gallinas mean- children only speak when spoken to...

Los pajaros tirandole a la escopeta - the pig huffing at the wolf

Mas rapido se coge a un mentiroso que a un cojo - quicker to catch a liar than a gimp

Mas sabe el diablo por viejo que por diablo - the devil is wiser for being old than for being the devil

Mas vale malo conocido que bueno por conocer - better the devil you know

Mas vale pajaro en mano que cien volando - bird in hand is better than two in the bush (as above)

Mono vestido de seda sigue siendo mono - monkey dressed in silk is still a monkey

Niño que no llora no mama - squeaky wheel gets the oil

No hay mal que por bien no venga - everything happens for a reason

No se puede escupir para arriba - can't piss against the wind

Para abajo todos los santos ayudan - it's easy going down

Para atrás ni para coger impulso - there's no going back

Que por mí no quede ... - i've done all I can...

Recoge tu serpentina que se acabo tu carnaval - your time is up; wore out your welcome

Se va a coger el culo con la puerta y la nariz con la ventana - going to slice his nose to spite his face

Si no la caga a la entrada, la caga a la salida - if he doesn't screw up on the way in, he'll screw up on the way out

Siempre hay un roto para un descosido - there is a lid for every pot

Chapter 5

Now What?

Use it or lose it! As you can see, I did leave out certain words and expressions of extreme obcenity and vulgarity; no need for those here. As we may or

may not have noticed, depending on circumstances and location, that the "cuban" spoken today is very different from the "cuban" we grew up with speaking. I did not include those more current expressions here.

I hope you continue to enjoy this little piece of our culture, and treasure it like I do.

Please pass it on to all your relatives and friends so

everyone can have this precious record of our unique verbal expression.

Peace and Love! Hasta lueguito!!!

www.ingramcontent.com/pod-product-compliance
Lightning Source LLC
Chambersburg PA
CBHW020518030426
42337CB00011B/443